Three Weeks to Freedom
A Daily Devotional Study of Philemon

Argle Smith

Scripture quotations taken from the Holy Bible, New Living Translation, Copyright ©1996, 2004. Used by permission of Tyndale House Publishers, Inc., Wheaton, Illinois 60189. All rights reserved.

ISBN-13: 978-1973808862

Day One
Clearing a Path to Freedom

You know, many Christians today can't find a moment in their busy lives to study the Word of God. We are bombarded with so many activities, and the advancement of technology has made life difficult to manage our time well. We have so much on our overwhelmed plates that it seems impossible to add one more thing. However, if the Bible is not on your main dish, you are not eating right. We have to make room to study Scripture. So, let's start now.

Scrape some of that junk food that's going to end up killing you off of your plate, and join me as we begin to study the epistle of Philemon. I challenge you to bring God's Word into your life each day, and I want to make that possible to you.

The letter of Philemon is found in the New Testament. It is only one chapter long, consisting of 25 verses.

Philemon was written by the Apostle Paul. Therefore, before we study Philemon, we need a little background information about its author. The Apostle Paul was once a Jewish religious leader. His name was Saul before being changed by the Church. His previous career was to hunt down and arrest Christians, who were spreading rapidly throughout the world. Paul oversaw the arrests and even executions of many believers (Acts 7:7-8:1; 9:1-2).

All that changed quickly for Paul when, one day on a road to Damascus, he was confronted by the risen Lord Jesus Christ (Acts 9:4-6). This encounter eventually led to Paul's remarkable conversion. At first, the Christians had a difficult time believing that this man, who had been killing and imprisoning them, was truly a follower of Jesus. But Paul's spiritual transformation was for real, and Paul soon climbed up the ranks in the Church, eventually earning the title of Apostle. The Apostles carried the highest authority in the first century Church.

Paul was called to be an Apostle to the Gentiles, which is anyone besides a Jew. Paul understood that salvation was for absolutely everyone. Paul taught, "There is no longer Jew, or Gentile, slave or free, male and female. For you are all one in Christ Jesus" (Galatians 3:28). Paul fought for the equality of all believers under the headship of the Lord Jesus Christ.

Eventually, like many of his companions, Paul was imprisoned for his faith. While in prison, Paul wrote several epistles (letters), including Philemon. Tomorrow we will begin the journey in this short but rich letter.

1. What could you sacrifice from your busy life to make room for God's word?
2. How would your life look different if you let Jesus come into your deepest areas?
3. Would you be willing, like Paul, to suffer in chains for Jesus Christ?

Day Two
Chained for God

"This letter is from Paul, a prisoner for preaching the Good News about Christ Jesus, and from our brother Timothy" (Verse 1a).

As I have already said, the Apostle Paul wrote this letter from prison. He was in chains for preaching the Gospel, which is the Good News about Jesus Christ. The Gospel is the message of Jesus Christ, our Savior. Jesus is God's Son sent to earth through the young virgin, Mary, to live a perfect life.

His mission was to freely offer his blameless body as a substitution sacrifice for our sinful bodies. The Bible summarizes the Gospel by saying, "For God loved the world so much that he gave his one and only Son, so that anyone who believes in him will not perish but have eternal life" (John 3:16).

Timothy was Paul's young disciple. He was born to a Jewish mother and a Greek father in Lycaonion, which was a small area in what is now Turkey (Asia Minor). As the Apostle to the Gentiles, Paul took several mission trips during his lifetime. Sometime during his second mission trip, he met and converted Timothy. He became one of Paul's companions on his missionary adventures, along with Silas.

Timothy's mother, Eunice, and grandmother, Lois, also converted to Christianity, and earned great respect in the Church. Timothy eventually became the bishop of the Ephesus Church, but he did accompany Paul while he was in prison.

Paul was a spiritual father to Timothy. We are all somewhere along the path of our Christian faith. Some of us are more mature than others. One of the commandments for all believers is that we go and make disciples (Matthew 28:16-20).

All of us should have a Paul in our lives—someone we look up to as a spiritual mentor, someone who has walked further and experienced more in the faith than us. Likewise, we should be looking for our Timothy—someone we can mentor through our experiences, someone we can lead by example in the faith.

1. How do we present the Gospel with those around us?
2. Who is your Paul?
3. Who is your Timothy?

Day Three
One in Christ Jesus

"I am writing to Philemon, our beloved co-worker, and to our sister Apphia, and to our fellow soldier Archippus, and to the church that meets in your house" (Verses 1b and 2).

Paul had written a letter from prison in Rome to Colossae, a town in Asia Minor (modern-day Turkey). This was by far, Paul's shortest letter. It would have been written on a single piece of papyrus. Paul honors Philemon by calling him a co-laborer. We notice right away that Philemon was probably a well-off person. He had a church in his home, which only wealthier people could accommodate. Nearly all Christians met in a home church for the first three centuries because they either could not afford to build or were not permitted to build. The house had to be a large enough estate to hold many people.

Paul listed a few of the prominent people in his home church, but as we will soon see, this letter was specifically for Philemon. Apphia was probably Philemon's wife, and some think Archippus was his son. They were both a part of the larger Church in Colossae (Colossians 4:9,17).

Today, we have the privilege of being a part of a 2000-year-long rich Church tradition. We have fully established Church leadership, doctrine, liturgy, places of worship, etc. We have the kinks worked out. However, this was not the case for the early Church.

When we study the different church fellowships in the New Testament, the way they practiced varied widely. The Bible provides for us a descriptive, not prescriptive, guide for Church practice. This means that while we have ideas on how Church should be done from Scripture, we do not have something set in stone.

We don't know exactly how Church is supposed to be. That's why Church can get messy, and this is one reason why many Churches are vastly different in practice today. But the truth is, there is only one universal Church. Christ is the head of the Church, regardless of how each body looks or practices their faith.

1. In what ways can all of us contribute to our local church—from the richest to the poorest members?

2. How is your church fellowship similar or different from that of the early Church?

3. How can we seek unity in love with other believers who adhere to different church practices from your own?

Three Weeks to Freedom

Day Four
The High Price of Adoption

"May God our Father and the Lord Jesus Christ give you grace and peace" (Verse 3).

This greeting was Paul's customary greeting that he included in all of his letters. Paul even included this greeting in Galatians, which had a more reprimanding tone. This greeting is a blessing. What better way to begin a conversation with someone than to bless them!

Most people speed read over the greetings, but let's reflect on what Paul was saying. First of all, he said we are God's children because Paul called God, "our Father." If you are a believer, the Bible teaches that you have been adopted as a son or daughter of the Most High God.

Galatians is just one very fitting passage we can look at concerning our adoption:

> But when the right time came, God sent
> his Son, born of a woman, subject to the
> law. God sent him to buy freedom for
> us who were slaves to the law, so that he
> could adopt us as his very own children.
> And because we are his children, God
> has sent the Spirit of his Son into our
> hearts, prompting us to call out, "Abba,
> Father." Now you are no longer a slave
> but God's own child. And since you are
> his child. God has made you his heir
> (Galatians 4:4-7).

What a remarkable passage of Scripture! We were once slaves, but God bought our freedom so that he could adopt us as his children.

Next, Paul called Jesus, the "Lord." In Greek, this word is *Kurios*, which normally means Master or Lord. It carries a meaning of authority. The Bible teaches that all authority has been given to Jesus (Matthew 28:18). And because our freedom has been purchased by the blood of Jesus, we owe him our lives. He is our Master now. That is what the cliché means, "Making Jesus the Lord of your life." This means, as believers, we are not in charge anymore. We have to obey Jesus' direction for our lives.

Now Paul declared in our Philemon verse that we receive two things from Father God and Jesus; grace and peace. Sometimes Paul added the word mercy to the greetings. Many don't understand the difference between grace and mercy. Very simply, mercy is not getting what you deserve. The Bible says that we deserve death and eternal damnation, but when we were adopted as children we received mercy. Meaning we have been saved from that judgment.

On the other hand, grace is getting what you don't deserve. We don't deserve any of the blessings from God. We don't deserve adoption, redemption, salvation, etc. We cannot earn or work for God's grace. Grace is free, and it can't be bought. You don't have enough to pay for it anyway because the cost of grace is high, it's the price of Jesus' sinless blood poured out for you on the cross. You can only receive grace. So be grateful.

Finally, there is peace. The Bible says our peace comes from God, and is delivered to us through the Holy

Spirit. The Holy Spirit gives peace that surpasses understanding (Philippians 4:7). If your heart is heavy and troubled let Him grace you with peace. Remember to greet one another with a blessing today, and receive the peace, grace, and mercy that comes from God the Father, his Son, and the Holy Spirit.

1. How much does it cost to be God's child?
2. What area of your life do you need to surrender to the Lord Jesus Christ?
3. How can we be a blessing to those around us?

Day Five
Lifted on a Prayer

"I always thank my God when I pray for you, Philemon, because I keep hearing about your faith in the Lord Jesus and your love for all of God's people" (Verses 4 and 5).

As was the Jewish custom, Paul probably kept regular times of prayer each day for approximately two hours or more a day. Here we see that when Paul prayed for Philemon, he specifically gave thanks for his most prominent godly characteristics; faith and love.

These are great examples of the fruit of the Spirit. The greatest characteristics a believer can strive for is faith, hope, and love (Corinthians 13:13). Paul often began his letters with such flattering words of encouragement. Why? Because he was about to challenge Philemon with a favor, and Paul was trying to win him over. Philemon was obviously not a selfish Christian.

There is a lesson to be had here: When we pray for someone, a part of our prayer should be dedicated to giving thanks for the person's more positive characteristics. Sometimes we like to just pray for the person to change. Also, I feel it is important for us to encourage one another with words of affirmation. We hear so much about how we've messed up, and sometimes it helps to hear what we're doing right. God is a big proponent of encouragement and affirmation. So, let me end with this prayer:

> Father God, I am so thankful for those participating in this study who have the desire to bring more of your Word into their life. May this study be both a blessing and an encouragement for them. May my contributions glorify you and your Kingdom. Illumine their hearts with the light and joy from the Holy Spirit. In the name of your Son, Jesus Christ. Amen.

1. What priority does prayer have in your life?
2. How can you affirm and encourage others?
3. Are you ready to be challenged further by God?

Day Six
Being Generous with God's Provisions

"And I am praying that you will put into action the generosity that comes from your faith as you understand and experience all the good things we have in Christ" (Verse 6).

At first glance, this verse may appear simple, but it is very compact. We already saw how the Apostle Paul flattered Philemon by complementing him on his two best attributes; faith and love. Now we see Paul subtly beginning to challenge Philemon.

Paul said he was praying for something very specific for Philemon. Paul wanted to see Philemon's faith in action. Faith is not stagnant. In the book of James, it says multiple times, "Faith is dead without good works" (James 2:14-26). Our faith produces good works in us. Sometimes the work produced through our faith is called fruit. The fruit Paul specifically prayed for Philemon was generosity. The Bible says "For God loves a person who gives cheerfully" (2 Corinthians 9:7).

Paul also explained in the Philemon passage that when we experience and understand all the good things we have in Jesus Christ, it makes us so much more likely to be generous. We have a rich inheritance that we are heirs to (Ephesians 1:11-14). We will enter into glory someday and see all the rich blessings our salvation has provided.

But even now on earth, we must understand that, "Whatever is good and perfect comes down to us from God our Father" (James 1:17). And everything we possess belongs to God. We are just stewards of his belongings. And when we finally realize this, we become more generous.

I love Psalm 50:10-12:

> For all the animals of the forest are mine,
> and I own the cattle on a thousand hills. I
> know every bird on the mountains, and
> all the animals of the field are mine. If I

were hungry, I would not tell you, for all
the world is mine and everything in it.

It is hard not to be generous when we see how generous
God is with us.

1. What ways do you need to put your faith into action?
2. What is preventing you from being more generous?
3. How has God been generous to you?

Day Seven
This Will Only Hurt a Little

"Your love has given me much joy and comfort, my brother, for your kindness has often refreshed the hearts of God's people" (Verse 7).

Yesterday we saw that Paul was praying for Philemon's faith to be put into action through generosity. However, we see from this verse today that Philemon was already a generous man. Therefore, we can assume that Paul was going to ask a favor of Philemon that goes well beyond Philemon's comfort level of generosity that he was accustomed to.

Paul refers to Philemon as a brother, someone he feels a close bond with. Philemon seemed to be a person Paul was comfortable talking to. Paul said he felt joy at the amount of love Philemon poured out on the other believers. When Paul talked about the hearts being refreshed through Philemon, Paul was referring to Philemon's hospitality.

Hospitality was heavily stressed in this culture. It's wonderful how Philemon had opened his home to the believers. This was no small task. This level of hospitality took someone with the financial means to be able to handle a home church: someone with a large enough estate, who had laborers, and someone who could provide the food to feed them, especially for the poorer believers.

So yes, Philemon was a very generous man. But as we are about to discover, Paul is going to ask Philemon to stretch his generosity even further. Sometimes God wants us to exercise our gifting even beyond what we think we are capable of. Even if you are using your giftings, God may want you to go beyond your comfort level. His vision for us is often bigger than what we can imagine.

1. How is God wanting to stretch you beyond your comfort zone?
2. What can you do to be more hospitable?
3. What are God's plans and vision for your life?

Day Eight
Sir, Yes Sir!

"That is why I am boldly asking a favor of you. I could demand it in the name of Christ because it is the right thing for you to do" (Verse 8).

Wow! All flattery aside, now it's time for Paul to get to it. But first let's point out the "That is why" part. Paul felt that he could boldly ask for this favor because of everything we've talked about from verses four through seven: Philemon had a lot of faith, love, and generosity, and Paul had a close bond with Philemon.

At the same time, Paul wanted Philemon to understand his position of authority. Philemon came from a high social class, which was valued in his culture. Let's say that Philemon was probably not used to taking orders. However, Paul was the founder or spiritual father of the Church there. He was an Apostle. Spiritual authority trumps social status (remember this point). Paul wanted

Philemon to understand that he was asking as a friend, but he could have ordered him as his superior.

Paul was saying the favor that he was about to ask of Philemon was the right thing to do, and something Philemon ought to do. Or in other words, Paul shouldn't even have to ask because Philemon should do it without being told.

Sometimes we get used to living according to certain social and cultural customs. And because we don't give our behavior much thought, we don't change. But sometimes our social and cultural habits are wrong, and we ought to change. There is a societal status quo, but there is a higher spiritual standard that we should always be striving for.

1. What type of spiritual leader was Paul?
2. What areas of your life ought to be brought under spiritual authority?
3. Which higher spiritual standards of personal holiness should you be striving for?

Day Nine
Humor an Old Man

"But because of our love, I prefer simply to ask you. Consider this as a request from me—Paul, an old man and now also a prisoner for the sake of Christ Jesus" (Verse 9).

Yesterday we saw how Paul reminded Philemon of his spiritual authority that he had over Philemon and his church, since Paul was the one who fathered the church as an Apostle. Paul was about to ask Philemon for a challenging favor—something that would push Philemon's giftings to their limits. But before Paul asked the favor, he backed up a little. Paul did not want to have to force Philemon to obey his request. But Paul wanted Philemon to respond out of the love and respect of their friendship.

Paul was now an old man, suffering in chains for the cause of Jesus Christ. How could anyone not grant this elderly man a request for all he has suffered and endured for the Church and the Gospel? Paul had given up everything, including his physical freedom, for Jesus.

People respected their elders in this culture. Since Paul converted, he had been whipped several times, faced death many times, received the 39 lashes at least five times, beaten with rods at least three times, was stoned at least once, was shipwrecked at least three times, has been robbed, has gone hungry and thirsty, has been through the cold, and now he is facing death in Rome (2 Corinthians 11:7-33). How could Philemon say no? What is this grand request going to be?

1. If Paul wrote you a similar letter, would you be able to say no to what he asked of you?
2. If God wrote you a letter asking a favor, would you say no? What is God asking of you lately?
3. Why should we respect our elders?

Day Ten
Ah Ha!

"I appeal to you to show kindness to my child, Onesimus. I became his father in the faith while here in Prison" (Verse 10).

So, we finally have gotten to the punch line. Paul's request was that Philemon shows Onesimus kindness. That doesn't sound so difficult. After all, Philemon's greatest attributes were love, faith, and generosity. We definitely need to know a little background information on Onesimus.

First of all, Onesimus was one of Philemon's household slaves. He had escaped. A slave, under Roman law, was both a person and property. Slavery was completely legal and accepted as a cultural norm. The head of the household even had the authority to execute his slaves.

Slaves made up a large part of the work force. They were able to work for their eventual freedom. Some freed slaves even became wealthy. Onesimus was a household slave. Household slaves were much better off than most other slaves, like mining slaves for example.

Everyone agreed in this culture that slaves were people, but no one argued that slaves should be free. Educated male slaves, like Onesimus, would be sent on errands. Some of these slaves took this opportunity to escape, like Onesimus had done (Keener p. 643).

The slave had to get far away. Onesimus made it all the way to Rome. Onesimus probably took Philemon's property and money with him, thus committing theft. The slave himself was considered stolen property, thus anyone harboring a slave was guilty of being in possession of stolen property (Keener p. 643).

Philemon would have had to purchase another slave to replace Onesimus. Therefore, when a slave was captured, the punishment was very severe. Roman law required that a captured slave be returned (Keener p. 644). Therefore, Paul returned Onesimus to Philemon.

We don't know the whole story, but we know that somehow Onesimus came into contact with Paul in Rome, and Paul led Onesimus to the Lord Jesus. Onesimus was no longer a slave to the world, but a child of God; an heir to the Father. Paul was now Onesimus' spiritual father. But by law, Paul had to send Onesimus back. Although, he does not send Onesimus back empty handed. Paul gave Onesimus this letter signed in his own name.

The first request was for Philemon to show kindness to Onesimus. We are about to discover just how kind Paul wants Philemon to be. Stay tooned!

1. What aspects of our culture today is legal but maybe not moral or ethical?
2. Is there someone you need to show kindness to, but that's easier said than done?
3. How can we, like Paul, stand up for the social justice issues of our day?

Day Eleven
Welcome Home Brother

"Onesimus hasn't been of much use to you in the past, but now he is very useful to both of us" (Verse 11).

Paul made a pun—Onesimus' name means useful. The wealthier class had a stereotype that slaves were lazy. Paul was saying that Onesimus was not very useful to Philemon as a slave, but as a child of God, he could be very useful to the Church.

We can start to see the argumentation that Paul was using. He was attempting to get Philemon to change his perspective concerning Onesimus from that of a slave (property) to that as a brother in Christ. Now we can barely begin to see were Paul was heading and understand just how this favor was really going to challenge Philemon to his core.

I grew up in a very poor family. I remember standing in line to receive government food and food stamps. I remember the embarrassment I felt at times when standing in line at the grocery store checkout. But we were not poor because my parents were lazy. Far from it. My dad worked two jobs and my mother worked one job and raised us kids at the same time. Many times, at Christmas we would receive help from the Salvation Army and my church. If it weren't for this help, we would have gone without. We must never jump to conclusions when we see people living in poverty. We just don't know how they got into that situation.

1. How can we make those in our church, who are from different social classes, feel like family?

2. What are the negative stigmatisms that we have today concerning people living in poverty?

3. What perspectives do you have concerning the poor that you want to change?

Day Twelve
Torn Apart

"I am sending him back to you, and with him comes my own heart" (Verse 12).

Paul was explaining that when he viewed Onesimus as a son in the faith, he actually loved and cared about him as a person. It was not an easy choice—sending Onesimus back to Philemon. There was a risk that Onesimus would be in danger from Philemon. Paul wanted Philemon to be kind to Onesimus (Verse 10).

Paul knew that Philemon was in his legal rights to severely beat or execute Onesimus. Imagine sending your child, who you loved and cared for, to his possible death. Imagine how torn you would be. The decision might not have been Paul's to make. Onesimus might have been torn away from Paul. During this period, there were hired men, similar to bounty hunters, that would go out and search for escaped slaves. It's possible that Onesimus was discovered and returned by one of these bounty hunters, under the direction of Philemon. We simply do not know.

There is a clue that maybe Onesimus was captured and placed in the jail with Paul because Paul, in the original Greek, literally says Onesimus was "born" in prison (Verse 10). Paul delivered Onesimus into this his new faith. What divine providence that Onesimus would end up in the same cell as Paul!

God has you where you are in this life for a reason. I don't know what your current situation is, but I do know that God wants you to be a parent; if not a physical, then spiritual. God wants you to raise up children in the faith—children who will one day leave you for one reason or another. It's our Job to raise these children in the way they should go (Proverbs 22:6).

1. Who has God recently brought into your life?
2. How has God helped you get through challenging circumstances?
3. Why does God have you where you are right now in life?

Day Thirteen
Shedding Light

"I wanted to keep him here with me while I am in these chains for preaching the Good News, and he would have helped me on your behalf" (Verse 13).

Today we are halfway through the Philemon study. It is now clear what Paul was asking Philemon. He was asking for Philemon to give Onesimus his freedom. What a picture we have here! Paul was in chains for preaching the Gospel. He was asking for Onesimus to be freed so that he could serve the Church. More specifically, so he could assist Paul in prison. Paul was making the argument that if Philemon freely decided to free his slave, then it would appear that Philemon was doing this generous act out of his love for Paul and faith in God.

No one in Paul's day had even come close to doing what Paul had just done. You don't simply suggest to someone to release their slave. Many slaveholders in the

US, before the Civil War, did not want their slaves to hear the Gospel message. They feared that if their slave was born again, then they would be forced to free the slave, based upon Philemon (Keener p. 643). This letter packs a mighty punch for the equality of mankind.

God's word has a way of shedding light into the dark places of our culture. The Apostle John explained that, "God is light and there is not darkness in him at all" (1John 1:5). He said elsewhere that, "The light shines in the darkness and the darkness can never extinguish it" (John 1:5). And we know that the "Light of the World" is Jesus (John 8:12). That light shines bright in followers of Christ. We must let that light penetrate into all the dark places of our world.

1. Is God calling upon you to change your views about our culture upside down?
2. We all have biases and false beliefs that God is trying to illuminate. What part of your mind is God pouring his truth into?
3. How can we change the social justice issues of our day?

Day Fourteen
You Are Free to Go

"But I didn't want to do anything without your consent. I wanted you to help because you were willing, not because you were forced" (Verse 14).

Yesterday, we saw Philemon challenged by Paul to free Onesimus for the ministry of the Church, especially to assist Paul in prison. Today, Paul subtly reminded Philemon again of his authority over Philemon as the founding Apostle of his church. Paul was saying that as an Apostle, he had the authority to free Onesimus himself. However, he was giving Philemon the opportunity to make the right choice. It's like when you give your toddler to the count of three.

It is clear at this point in the letter that Paul had already freed Onesimus. Philemon doesn't really have a choice, at least a choice that isn't pressured. He was in a position that would be extremely difficult to say no.

First, Paul has publicly announced that Philemon is a generous and faithful man. The peer pressure was on. Second, it was Paul, the aged persecuted Apostle in chains, saying I would already have done this because it's the right thing to do (vv. 8,9). Basically, Paul was saying, I have the authority to either order you, or free him myself, but I'm giving you a chance. And then, there were the witnesses (vv. 1,2,23,24). The letter was public. It was written to the entire Church. People were watching!

Granted, Paul was tricky. He was a master of argumentation and rhetoric. But what Paul did was not attempting to be merely manipulative, because underneath it all, Paul simply wanted what was best for Onesimus, Philemon, and the Church. Paul's heart was to see true unity, equality, and family in the Church. The Church was meant to be freed by Christ.

True unity and equality between our brothers and sisters in Christ cannot be achieved without real freedom— both physical and spiritual. The beauty of the Church is that we are all one in Christ, through Christ, and under Christ.

1. What does Jesus' words mean to you, "So if the Son sets you free, you are truly free" (John 8:36)?

2. Name a time that you were placed in a position that was extremely difficult to say no.

3. How can we work towards unity, equality, and family in the universal Church today?

Day Fifteen
Raising the Bar

"It seems Onesimus ran away for a little while so that you could have him back forever. He is no longer like a slave to you. He is more than a slave, for he is a beloved brother, especially to me. Now he will mean much more to you, both as a man and as a brother in the Lord" (Verses 15 and16).

Paul was concluding his letter to Philemon. As I pointed out, Philemon (as a believer) does not have a choice but to free Onesimus. But Paul wants him to understand why. Onesimus could no longer be Philemon's slave because he was a Christian. Onesimus was a son of God. Which in fact, made him Philemon's spiritual brother. You cannot enslave your family, especially your brother.

Paul was pointing out that, though it was wrong for Onesimus to run away, it was better for Philemon in the end. As a household slave, Onesimus probably would have earned his freedom and left. But now, as a family member, Philemon had Onesimus forever. Paul once said, "And we know that God causes everything to work together for the good of those who love God and are called according to his purpose for them" (Romans 8:28).

Philemon had only one choice now, which was to free Onesimus. Philemon had no justification as a believer to keep Onesimus as a slave. He can only appeal to the Roman law, but Christians are held to a much higher standard: the law of Jesus Christ (Galatians 6:2, 1 Corinthians 9:21, etc.).

1. Does your church feel like a family?
2. How can we better view fellow Christians as brothers and sisters?
3. What government laws are you holding onto to justify your actions that would be in violation of the law of Christ?

Day Sixteen
50/50

"So if you consider me your partner, welcome him as you would welcome me" (Verse 17).

Paul leaves no wiggle room for Philemon. Welcoming Onesimus as a free man and a brother in Christ was not enough. Paul told Philemon to welcome Onesimus as he would have welcomed Paul himself. And if there was any further confusion, he was to welcome Onesimus as he would a partner.

In a business, a partner normally owns half of the company. Paul was telling Philemon to recognize Onesimus as an equal. Wow! Talk about a change of perspective! That was what Paul meant when he said, "There is no longer Jew or Gentile, slave or free, male and female. For you are all one in Christ Jesus" (Galatians 3:28). Paul explained that, as God's children, we are coheirs with Jesus (Romans 8:17). We are all equal. With equality comes unity, and love binds them together. Jesus commanded the believers to love one another (John 15:17).

When we see our fellow believers as equal partners there is no room left for hate, unforgiveness, jealousy, greed, or envy. When we are equal, we can unite as one. We can start to forgive one another. We can begin to encourage one another. Most importantly, we can love one another. The Apostle John said, "No one has ever seen God. But if we love each other, God lives in us, and his love is brought to full expression in us" (1 John 4:12).

1. How can we start seeing other believers the way Paul wants us to and the way Jesus commanded us to?
2. What is preventing you from seeing your fellow believers as equal?
3. How can we love more profoundly?

Day Seventeen
Priceless

"If he has wronged you in any way or owes you anything, charge it to me. I PAUL, WRITE THIS WITH MY OWN HAND: I WILL REPAY IT. And I won't mention that you owe me your very soul" (Verses 18 and19)!

Paul realized that there needed to be some reconciliation between Philemon and Onesimus. Philemon had been put out a lot of money and he had been betrayed by a slave he trusted to help run his estate. But Paul offered to repay it (or did he?).

Of course, Onesimus racked up quite the debt. He was probably a well-educated household slave. Thus, Philemon was out a lot of money.

1. $500 and up = Price today to cover stolen property and money that Onesimus used to get to Rome.
2. $40,000 = the equivalent cost today to replace Onesimus.

3. The debt of lost income or loss of services. And who knows what else.

But as Paul pointed out, Philemon owed Paul as well.

1. Priceless = The cost of your very soul! Ha-ha-ha!

Or in other words, Paul has already paid Onesimus' debt in full and then some. Here we see Paul at his clever argumentation shenanigans again. It's almost humorous.

This passage speaks volumes about forgiveness. Believers need to forgive each other's debts; whether that debt is monetarily tangible, a physical debt, or non-tangible debt, like an emotional debt.

1. Are you holding any debts over another believer's head that you need to forgive?
2. How much have you been forgiven by God?
3. What prevents forgiveness?

Day Eighteen
Saving Face

"Yes, my brother, please do me this favor for the Lord's sake. Give me this encouragement in Christ. I am confident as I write this letter that you will do what I ask and even more" (Verses 20 and 21)!

One last time Paul pleaded with Philemon to do the right thing. Again, as I have previously pointed out, Philemon did not really have a choice but to release Onesimus. So, if he had no choice then why did Paul keep talking like he did? That's the question I want to address today.

As Americans, we live in a Low-Context culture. This means we get straight to the point. We do not talk around the problem or issue. We use fewer words in a more efficient timely manner. If Paul were an American writing to Philemon the letter would have been even shorter than 25 verses. Paul would have written a private (not public) letter to Philemon saying that

Philemon must release Onesimus because it is the right and moral decision to make. Onesimus is a believer in Christ and you cannot enslave your brother. As a believer, you have to be able to forgive Onesimus and treat him as an equal. As the founder of Philemon's church, and with the Authority of an Apostle, Paul would have requested Onesimus to be sent back, if he would have sent him in the first place. Paul might have just kept Onesimus in Rome.

And that would have been the end of it unless Philemon refused. Then Paul would have had to take further measures—"short, sweet, and to the point." Paul still would have been respectable, but there would have been no doubt that this was an obligation and not a suggestion.

But this culture was not like the United States. This culture was a High-Context culture. This means the people talk around the issue or problem. It was considered impolite to be so direct. We call it "beating around the bush." They use more words in suggestive tones to talk about problems. Even though Paul was making requests, Paul was really not asking. Philemon knew exactly what Paul was saying, and he would have known he had no choice. People in High-Context cultures know how to "read between the lines."

So yes, like Paul, I am quite confident that Philemon did all he asked and even more. I am positive that Philemon had freed Onesimus and allowed him to return to Paul well supplied. There is no doubt in my mind.

I must add this because it's so significant. Saving face was extremely important in this culture. By Paul asking "favors," he was allowing Philemon to publicly save face. Even though Philemon has no choice, it appears publicly that the choice was his, and that Philemon made this decision out of his love, generosity, and great faith—the three attributes Paul ascribed to Philemon.

Who knows, maybe Paul was just reiterating what Paul knew Philemon was going to do all along. Maybe Philemon was going to do all of this with tremendous joy. But I have my suspicions that this was a humbling choice that Philemon had to really trust God for the strength to carry out.

1. What is God speaking to you through these two verses today?

2. How can we help fellow believers save face?

3. What are some ways we can be more sensitive to people from different cultures?

Day Nineteen
Unanswered Prayer

"One more thing—please prepare a guest room for me, for I am hoping that God will answer your prayers and let me return to you soon" (Verse 22).

As the letter of Philemon closes, Paul expressed his heart. He was in prison in Rome for his faith. He was following the path God had placed before him—a path of suffering. Jesus once said his followers had to carry their cross (Matthew 16:24).

All the Christians had been praying for Paul's release. Paul missed his spiritual Children. He had expressed this in more than one of his prison letters. But those prayers were probably never answered. Philemon was written around AD 61. Paul was martyred about seven years later. As a Roman citizen, Paul was beheaded soon after he was released from prison.

Paul's life ended in a way similar to those Christians he had persecuted before he converted himself. But Paul was not afraid of death. He welcomed it.

> For to me, living means living for Christ, and dying is even better. But if I live, I can do more fruitful work for Christ. So I really don't know which is better. I'm torn between two desires: I long to go and be with Christ, which would be far better for me. But for your sakes, it is better that I continue to live. (Philippians 1:21-24)

1. How do we keep a strong faith when things turn out differently than we had prayed?
2. Are you carrying your cross?
3. How far are you willing to go for Jesus?

Day Twenty
Your Name Here

"Epaphras, my fellow prisoner in Christ Jesus, sends you his greetings. So, do Mark, Aristarchus, Demas, and Luke, my co-workers" (Verse 23 and 24).

Paul was sending his final greetings. He dropped a few names. Let's go through this list.

1. Epaphras was one of Paul's converts from the Colossae church (Colossians 1:7). Everyone in Philemon's house church had probably been praying for him as well, since Paul described him as a fellow prisoner.

2. Mark was a very common name like Bill or Bob. We have no idea which Mark, Paul was referring to, but he was someone the church was very familiar with. This Mark could have been the author of the second Gospel Account. Mark the Evangelist, as he was called, was martyred by

pagan worshipers by being dragged through the streets with a roped tied around his neck.

3. Aristarchus was from Thessalaonica. He was another prisoner with Paul (Colossians 4:10). He traveled with Paul on many of his journeys. He was also eventually martyred for the faith.

4. Demas was one of Paul's companions from Thessalaonica as well. He traveled around with Paul. We learn that Demas eventually abandoned Paul because he loved the world too much (Timothy 4:10). However, he may have eventually come back.

5. And of course, there is Luke. He was the author of Luke and Acts. He was a Physician who accompanied Paul as an evangelist. Luke was eventually martyred by being hung in an olive tree for his faith.

Each person was willing to risk suffering, prison, or death for the Gospel of Jesus. (With the exception of Demas having his crisis of faith.) All of these men believed they possessed the absolute truth about God and our eternal destination, which they were willing to die for.

1. What are you willing to risk for Jesus and the Gospel?
2. How do you want to be remembered?
3. How much time do you regularly spend actively reaching the lost for Jesus?

Day Twenty-one
Free at Last

"May the grace of the Lord Jesus Christ be with your spirit" (Verse 25).

Today we end our study of Philemon. I am so glad you came along with me. For 21 days, we have uncovered the rich meaning of this letter verse-by-verse. We have seen Paul's heart. We have seen Philemon's battle. And we have seen Onesimus' radical transformation in Christ.

During this study, I gave many reasons to believe that Onesimus was freed and returned to help Paul in his Roman prison. But today I have one more reason to believe. That reason is that after 2000 years, you and I are still reading this letter. If Philemon had not freed Onesimus, this letter would not have been preserved. But because Onesimus was freed, this letter was copied and delivered to the bodies of Christ scattered throughout the Roman world.

The earliest surviving fragment of Philemon is called Papyrus 87 from around the year AD 250. This little book packs a big punch. The early Church believed it was important enough to hand copy and spread it all around. And our Apostolic Church Fathers believed it was important enough to include in the Canon of Scripture.

Paul ends with a blessing for Philemon, and so do I. I am so thankful for all of you who have joined me on this journey through Philemon. May the Holy Spirit fill you with joy and peace as you continue to follow in the steps of Jesus Christ, and seek God's Word. God bless!

1. What are your biggest take-aways from Paul's letter to Philemon?
2. What goals have you set for yourself as a result of this study?
3. What does the letter of Philemon add to Scripture?

Works Cited

Holy Bible: New Living Translation. Tyndale, Wheaton, Illinois. 1996.

Keener, Craig. *IVP Bible Background Commentary: New Testament.* InterVarsity Press, Downers Grove, Illinois. 1993.

Made in the USA
Middletown, DE
12 July 2024

57229346R00038